Visits to the Glade

Soul Connections

BRENDA BRUZON

with artwork from the Creative Sisters

Balboa Press books may be ordered through booksellers or by contacting:

Balboa Press
A Division of Hay House
1663 Liberty Drive
Bloomington, IN 47403
www.balboapress.com
1 (877) 407-4847

Because of the dynamic nature of the Internet, any web addresses or links contained in this book may have changed since publication and may no longer be valid. The views expressed in this work are solely those of the author and do not necessarily reflect the views of the publisher, and the publisher hereby disclaims any responsibility for them.

Any people depicted in stock imagery provided by Thinkstock are models, and such images are being used for illustrative purposes only. Certain stock imagery © Thinkstock.

ISBN: 978-1-5043-4479-1 (sc)
ISBN: 978-1-5043-4480-7 (e)

Library of Congress Control Number: 2015918713

Print information available on the last page.

Balboa Press rev. date: 12/18/2015

BALBOA.
PRESS
A DIVISION OF HAY HOUSE

To all my creative sisters, everywhere.

Contents

Acknowledgements

I would like to thank the following people for their wise teaching and support. *Visits to the Glade* is my tribute to you all.

Gill Edwards, for all her books, especially *Stepping Into the Magic* and *Living Magically*[1], which taught me how to access my inner wisdom through visualisation. My counsellor, Sally-Ann Soulsby, for helping me to unravel my past, thus freeing me to live in the present and find my own way; for introducing me to the work of Gill Edwards; and for the remarkable matrix re-imprinting sessions[2]. William Bloom, for *The Endorphin Effect* book[3] and workshop that I attended in 2014. William's visualisation techniques, combined with Gill Edwards' enabled me to experience *The Fledgling and the Dancer*. My friends Farzaneh and Hamid Safari and their daughter Niloufar, for allowing me to include *Arman Safari* in this account. Wenche Krag Beard, Sally-Ann (again) and Sarah French, for believing in me and seeing my light before I ever knew it was there. Wenche (again), Naomi Seager, Olga Oakenfold, Jane Dancey and Safia Bowley, for teaching me yoga and leading me to meditation, the foundations of my awakening to spirit. My spiritual teachers – Gill Edwards (of course), Deepak Chopra, Neale Donald Walsch, Eckhart Tolle, Louise Hay, William Bloom (again) and Jane Roberts for the Seth books, to name my most important guides to date. Thank you all for 'pointing at the moon'[4]; thank you for helping me to remember what I've always known. Pam Hardy and Chrissie Hearn, for healing and for confirming my life's purpose and path. My spiritual sisters, the ladies of 'Spirituality Club', who have been journeying with me these past three years. The Creative Sisters for their artistic contributions, acknowledgement, encouragement and support. Natasha Duursma for the art photography. Lucille Mari, Barb Carter and the Balboa Press team for holding my hand through my first adventure into publishing. And of course, my friends and family, who have supported me during this period of great change, my 'mid-life crisis'. And especially my husband, David Hammond, for his unfailing love and support, even though he's not quite sure he 'believes in it'.

Introducing the Glade

Where is *the Glade*? *The Glade, my* glade, is in every wood, in every forest I have ever walked in, and in none.

I have always loved trees, always loved walking in woodland. To walk and sit, ponder and listen. Any season any day. Variations in light, colour, texture, smell and sound make every visit unique. Dappled light, the sunbeams through the trees. Spring growth, so excitingly bright and juicy. Birdsong and woodland noise. Robins, blackbirds, pigeons and crows. The occasional delight of an owl, a cuckoo or woodpecker. Scrabbling, leaping squirrels, cursing from the treetops at the dogs that chase them. Welcome leafy shade in summer's heat. Rain, hindered at first from its descent, breaking through in unexpected plops and splashes. Squelchy sounds where boots tread. Fairy pools that gather in tree-root hollows and where branches fork. The pungent smell of fungus and mould, muddy earth and wet bark, dripping. Damp soil and rotting leaves becoming one. Fluffy lichen on knobbly bark, springy underfoot. Autumn foliage, yellow, brown, orange, red, weaving a soft crumpled carpet. Crunching crackly twigs. Whispering leaves, shivering in light breeze. Creaking tree-limbs, groaning with the rumbling wind above. But where I walk, such stillness. The trees protecting me.

I think I must have a deep many-lifetimes connection to trees and woodland. I feel unsettled without trees. I like to be amongst them wherever I live, work and play. I walk in the woods close to our home almost every day with our dog, Fig. My husband, Dave, often comes too. When I met Dave he was a tree surgeon. He had worked with trees all his adult life and spent his childhood in their branches. A naughty schoolboy throwing acorns at passing cars. I like to call Dave my tree-fella. Perfect synchronicity, the coming together of tree-lovers.

The Glade in these accounts is not an actual place, but one that I have found both in and out of my mind. It is where I go during meditation and visualisation. A place of my own making, so dear to my heart. My place of safety and retreat. *The Glade* is where I go to meet my self in various forms, to ask for guidance and to pick up messages. For me, when I think of it and try to describe it, this place seems to occupy space hovering above my right shoulder. *The Glade* is where I access my higher wisdom, where I go to connect to spirit.

My mind does not direct these experiences. These encounters are not created by my conscious thoughts. Neither do they feel like day or night dreaming. When I go to *the Glade* I quiet my mind and let go. I receive.

To get to *the Glade* I always follow the same path. I find myself walking in the woods, following a thin rooty path through trees. I always turn right and walk towards a lighter area up ahead, to the left of me, that becomes clearer after a few moments. I go down a gentle slope and here is *the Glade* - a clearing in the trees where the light can shine down from the sky, where the sun or moon can be seen through a break in the canopy. *The Glade* is carpeted in soft grass, with leafy ferns around the edges. In the centre is a campfire with two long log-seats on either side. It is here that I meet my messengers, whoever or whatever they may be. Sometimes I have particular questions that relate to challenges I am facing at the time. *The Glade* provides me with answers. Sometimes the messengers just come of their own accord and are a complete surprise to me.

In *the Glade* I have experienced the gentle nature of my soul. The kind and ever-patient parent that we all want to have and be. *The Glade* has brought me acceptance of who I am and taught me to celebrate my own uniqueness, no matter what my outer-world circumstances might be. Through my visits to *the Glade* I am understanding my true nature and potential. I realise all is unfolding perfectly, and that I am a perfect being, just the way I am.

My experiences in *the Glade* started in December 2011. By this time I had been in counselling for over a year and I was starting to understand my self and find the freedom to connect to my spiritual nature. At the same time I was beginning to open up through yoga, meditation, reading spiritual works and attending related workshops.

These experiences do not come to me every time I meditate. They were most frequent early on in my awakening, between 2011 and 2013, when my consciousness was just starting to expand, just starting to show me that there was more 'to it' than my rational mind could understand. Nowadays the way that I connect to my higher wisdom has changed and I have these experiences more rarely.

To be honest, I wasn't even sure these techniques would work for me, but I thought I'd give them a try! One thing I have practiced for some time is to quieten the chatter of my mind and then, once I am really present and there is no more 'white noise', I 'just wait and see' what comes next. The visualisation techniques have enabled me to deepen my connection and receive in a most beautiful and wonderful way.

Amongst these accounts I have also chosen to include a few of my significant 'way-marker' dreams, and a memory, some would say past or 'other'-life experience, accessed through a session of matrix re-imprinting with my counsellor. I have chosen to include these because the deep realisations that have followed each of these events feel to me to be of the same kind, and of the same significance and clarity, as those that I have had in *the Glade*.

I have recounted these experiences in the order that it came to me to write them, rather than in their chronological order of occurrence. Where I thought it would be useful, I have used italics to explain the context of my connection experiences. Plain text describes the experience itself. I have chosen to recount the experiences in the present tense as for me they are always present.

I hope you will enjoy these glimpses of my spiritual journey.

The Old Man and the Butterfly

I follow the narrow path, heading deliberately to the clearing in the woods. I wonder if someone or something might be waiting for me. I have a question to ask, but I try not to have any expectation, just in case there is no message for me today.

As I draw nearer to *the Glade*, the light becomes brighter, but this is not the sunlight that sometimes dapples through the canopy – this is another kind of light. As I come to the edge of the trees I see a bright white oval-shaped glow, hovering just above the ground next to the sitting-log on the right. The brilliance must be over seven feet in height and four feet in width. It vibrates for a few seconds. Then, as I stand, staring at the glow, the light fades and there, on the log, sits a very old man, with white hair trailing down his back, a long white beard to his knees, dressed in light grey flowing robes.

"Are you God?" I ask.

"Yes I am," he replies, nodding slowly. "And so are you," he smiles, his eyes twinkling.

He indicates the log next to him, inviting me to sit.

I have a question that has been bothering me recently. I feel it is best to get straight to the point. I know that the Old Man won't mind my directness.

"How will I know when I'm on the right path?" I ask the Old Man.

He answers, just as directly, as if he is just waiting for my question. Which of course, he is.

"Throughout your life you will find yourself in many different places and there will be many choices to make. Your path will depend on your choices. This is how your life will unfold. You will choose your own path."

Frustrated a little by the Old Man's answer, I try again.

"But why can't I know *now* if the choices I make are the right ones?"

"Because your growth depends on the choices you make. If all was known from the start, there would be no growth. Choose from the heart, choose what feels right to you. Choose what ignites your passion. That is the way to choose the right path: the right path for *you*."

We sit in silence for a while, looking into the crackling fire, watching the dancing flames and the flight of the glowing embers lifting up up into the sky above us, riding the twisted ropes of curling smoke.

The Old Man speaks again, slowly and quietly. He speaks as if he were talking to himself, speaking to the flames.

"Maybe now, all you see ahead of you are the choices and possibilities that relate to your situation now. But remember, only a few days, weeks, months, even years ago, you didn't even know about your messengers in *the Glade*. You had different choices to make, other crossroads that brought you to this moment. And so it will always be. We do not know what lies ahead. We only know that we can choose the path we want to take when we get there. That is why nobody else can give you the answers. Or if they do they may not be *your* answers. Others may be able to point out possible choices at a point in time, but not the answers for *you*. Only *you* can choose the person you want to be in relation to any event."

He looks meaningfully into my eyes and nods again. His eyes are as soft and grey as his robes. As wise and as laughing as the stones.

Having answered my questions and delivered his message, the Old Man unfolds to his full height – much taller than any man I have ever seen, he towers over me. And then he starts to glow white. The glow grows brighter until I cannot see him anymore, just the dazzling white oval remains, hovering in front of the log where he'd been sitting. Then from the light emerges a beautiful giant purple and silver butterfly, with enormous wings. The Butterfly hovers for an instant by the log next to me and then slowly slowly flaps its huge powerful wings. I feel the rush of air with each wing-beat, but he doesn't disturb the flames or smoke. Up up he flies, above the fire and into the sky, up with the glowing embers, climbing the twisted ropes of curling smoke.

This experience in the Glade came to me early in 2014, a few days after I'd had my first ever psychic reading. I had found the reading very interesting, especially watching how the medium communicated with her advising spirits, but I wasn't convinced that a certain direction the psychic was suggesting that I follow was the right one for me. So I was looking for help in knowing how to make decisions – how to make the 'right' choices for me.

The Urchin and the Waterfall

I walk into the woods, along the narrow path between the trees and down the slope into the clearing. *The Glade* is dark and sombre today, with very little light coming from up above. The fire is out.

Sitting on the right-hand log-seat is a small child, perhaps five or six years old, with black messy hair and dressed in bulky, black clothes, all ripped like rags. The child's legs and arms are bare, thin and white, and covered in dirty smudges. I realise as I draw nearer that this raggedy urchin is in fact 'little me', Little Brenda. She looks down at her dirty bare feet, her eyes full of tears, smears down her face. I feel such sadness coming from my little self. My young face, so full of self-doubt, my eyes so full of fear! I am shocked and hurt to see them. I see such a lack of trust, such low self-confidence, loneliness and confusion. All my self-sabotaging thoughts of not *being* enough, not *knowing* enough and not being *good enough,* personified by this incredibly dejected Little Brenda on the log.

I sit down next to my little self and feel all the self-doubt and fear surge up from Little Brenda's heart into my own. Tears come into *my* eyes now, as I look down at my small self. Again I feel it, the loneliness, the sadness and the fear. I reach out and draw Little Brenda to me, enveloping her gently in my arms, holding her.

"It's OK," I say, trying to reassure my little self.

"We can trust. It is all going to be alright," I continue. "We are a beautiful stardust being. We can have whatever our heart desires. Do not be afraid anymore. Speak your truth, be true to yourself. Come out into the open. Be joyful. Be recognised in places of welcome, wholeness and acceptance. Communicate your heartfelt desires and fulfil your life's purpose."

I pull away a bit and look down at Little Me. She is smiling up at me now, her eyes still wet but laughing. We look into each other's eyes, the same eyes, a sense of utterly blissful knowing passes between us.

Then I see that Little Brenda is starting to glow white at her core, a shining light coming from deep within her in the centre of her chest and spreading all over her body and around her. And I am glowing too, from my heart's centre and then out, beyond my body. I hug Little Brenda to me again and our light merges into one, spreading all around us. I get up and walk out of *the Glade*, down a short track to a waterfall that lies beyond. Little Brenda is now a part of me, moving with me towards the water.

Still radiant, I step into the clear pool and wade across towards the waterfall on the far side. I am now waist-high in the sparkling water. I stand under the gentle cascades, facing out to look at the pool and woodland beyond. As the water falls softly and refreshingly on my head, my shoulders and down my back, the glow from my body starts to spread out and away from me, rolling away into the water in dancing white-light ripples. I move my hands in my own sparkling reflection, wriggling my fingers to make little splashes and waves of dancing light. The waterfall washes away my doubts and fears. All my low self-worth is gone. Only joyous shining light remains.

As my vision comes to an end, the message that comes to me is:

"That is me, in this world. I am already doing it!"

This experience came to me during meditation when I decided to try out 'Meeting the Struggler'[5], a visualisation technique explained in Gill Edwards' Stepping into the Magic.

Arman Safari

I walk through the trees, along the narrow path, and down the slope. It seems like a summer's day, perhaps late afternoon. The light in the clearing is a soft orange-gold. Not the glow from the fire, however, as the fire is out. A radiance from above that fills *the Glade* with warmth.

As I walk into *the Glade* I see a boy standing by the log-seat on the right. He looks about ten years old, has brown skin, dark hair and big brown eyes. I know him instantly! He is Arman Safari, the son of my good friend, Farzaneh. He looks so much like them all, Farzaneh, his father Hamid and sister Niloufar.

"Are you well?" I ask. "Are you OK?"

"Yes," he replies, grinning wide and laughing. "I am well. I am very happy." And then "Look! I am running! I am jumping!" he declares.

And as he says this, Arman turns and starts to jump on and off the log behind him. On and off, on and off he jumps. Each time lifting his legs high and flinging up his arms in a funny exaggerated fashion. Then he runs around the log, jumping on and off again in front of me. Laughing as he demonstrates just how happy and well he is. So much energy. So much obvious delight in his vitality, his strength and freedom of movement.

"Who are you with?" I ask Arman, when he stops moving for a moment.

"I am with Farzaneh. We are happy, we are all OK."

"Can I tell Farzaneh, *my* Farzaneh?" I ask. He understands my meaning.

Arman says that I can, and that he has already sent her signs. That my Farzaneh already knows. That there are signs that she has noticed but not told me about. But yes, I can tell Farzaneh. Tell her he is OK. They are OK.

And with that, Arman Safari turns and runs joyfully out of *the Glade*.

This experience came to me as a complete surprise, one December morning in 2013. After doing my yoga practice at home, I was in shivasana, the lying down relaxation pose that I do at the end of my practice. I decided to visit the Glade to see who might be there.

Arman Safari, the son of my dear friends Farzaneh and Hamid Safari, was born severely handicapped with Cockayne syndrome, a very rare genetic disorder that affected the development of his nervous system and growth, sight and hearing and brought about premature ageing. He died in 2006, aged three.

The Assassination

I am in a kitchen in a Victorian style terraced three storey house, with steps from the ground floor down to the road. In the kitchen is a bowl of delicious-looking freshly baked bread rolls and I see other food laid out on the kitchen surface. I am with Dave and my daughter Emily. I suddenly become aware that I am in some kind of danger. This wearies me, but I know I have to pack my bags and leave the house immediately, get out as soon as I can. I ask Emily to help me. I am particularly keen to take some bread rolls with us, at least!

The next thing I know I am returning to the house with Dave, going up the steps to the front door. I have forgotten something important and we are going back to retrieve it. Dave is ahead of me on my left. He opens the front door and starts to enter the house. A man appears from a room inside and stands briefly in the corridor. He is holding a gun, his arm straight out in front of him, finding his target. He strides past Dave towards me. I am still on the steps. I see the man and the determined cold look on his face. I say "Oh no," not in fear, but more of a sigh of recognition, a sort of "Oh no, it's now is it?" acceptance of the inevitable. I am not at all afraid. Just resigned to what I know is about to happen.

The man shoots me in the head, once on the left, once on the right. I fall backwards off the steps and end up lying on my back on the path. Dave runs to me. I am not in any pain - in fact I am feeling sort of blissful. But I see the distraught and panicked look on Dave's face as he sees my head and all the blood. He tries to lift me in his arms.

"It's OK," I say, to reassure him, and then "Have they made a right mess of me?"

Dave is crying as he holds me close.

"It's OK." I say again. "I will see you again. I will wait for you. We have work to do together you and I."

I am happy. I am calm. Full of love. It is just as it is meant to be and I know that. There is no sadness or pain. I know I am dying and it is OK. More than OK in fact – it is beautiful.

On awakening from this dream, I felt so calm and peaceful. I was awestruck by the beauty and absolute perfection of my experience.

I also had a keen awareness that this was no random killing. I had been gunned down by the powers-that-be because I was considered a trouble-maker. I was speaking my truth and people were listening and this went against the accepted norm at the time. A government 'hit' to shut me up, so to speak.

From the time of this dream I have had no fear of my own death. I also know that Dave and I are together for a reason in this lifetime, and that we have been and will be together in other lifetimes, other planes of existence. We have work to do together and we are doing that work right now, here, and wherever else we might be.

Meeting Suki

I am lying at the edge of a meadow of long grass, poppies and daisies, the warm sunshine dappled on me through the overhanging trees. I can hear birds singing and insects buzzing around me, visiting the flowers. I feel warm and relaxed. After a while, I get up and walk along the tree-line, to the left of the field. There is a path leading up a hill ahead of me. I follow the path up to a little turreted castle, perky like a folly. I approach the castle's huge wooden front door and go in. The entrance-hall is tiled black and white like a chess-board. The interior is that of a large luxurious house.

I start to explore the ground-floor rooms that lead off the hall. I open the door to a room on the right at the back of the castle. Standing in the middle is a black highly polished grand piano. Sitting on the piano is a small child, a girl with large dark eyes and short black hair in a spiked-up style. She is wearing denim dungarees and trainers. She looks like one of those Japanese manga-style cartoon characters, but in human form. Somehow I know that her name is Suki. She is Suki Manga.

Suki is very pleased to see me and swings her legs excitedly as I approach. She then jumps down off the piano and runs towards me laughing. She leaps into my arms and I catch her. I am surprised and delighted by this little person who is hugging me so tightly. We laugh together as we look into each other's eyes and there is some sort of recognition that passes between us, some sort of unspoken understanding. Then Suki jumps down.

We start a game of hide and seek, all around the ground floor of the castle. Suki runs and hides and I have to find her, but she doesn't hide properly. Each time she hides she peeps out giggling so that I see her, which fills her with absolute glee. She squeals with pleasure every time I find her, hugs me and then runs off to the next place. Suki seems like a child, but somehow I know that she is older, wise. A knowing little bundle of joy.

After a while, when it seems that we've exhausted all the hiding places, Suki takes me by the hand to the back of the house and through some large French windows. There is a wide stone veranda beyond, spanning the width of the castle. Outstretched in front of us is an enormous garden, formally laid out with ornamental topiary hedges. We walk down some stone steps, Suki still holding my hand and laughing happily. She is so little beside me, barely up to my waist. Her hand in mine so small and sweet. I walk, Suki skips, along a wide grass pathway, between two tall dark hedges that lead us like a corridor to another part of the garden. I am aware of the size of the estate extending beyond these hedges to the sides and in front of us.

Eventually I can see that the path leads to a large ornate stone fountain, set in the middle of a carved raised pond. The water spurts up several feet high at the centre, and falls back after forming a beautiful bubbling light-filled tree of glass. As we get nearer the effervescence subsides and just the calm sparkling waters remain. Suki takes me nearer and then I notice that there are people all around the pond, facing our way expectantly.

Suki turns to look up at me and says "Here they are. You see, here they *all* are."

And I see that the people around the pond are all the people that I treasure in my life, past and present. My family, my friends, my workmates. They are all there, smiling at me. It's like a 'This is Your Life'[6] surprise party. I feel so much love, so much welcome, so much absolute approval.

I 'awakened' with tears in my eyes, full of wonder and amazement. I felt a little overwhelmed too by this remarkable experience, but with an overall sense of Wow! That was fabulous! I am fabulous!

This is the first ever connection to my inner wisdom that I experienced when trying out Gill Edwards' visualisation technique 'Meeting Your Higher Self'[7], described in her book Stepping Into the Magic. I had this experience after a home yoga practice, when I was relaxing in shivasana.

The Mirrors

I am in a dark room, standing in front of a freestanding mirror where I can see my head and shoulders. The mirror itself has an ornate burnished gold frame and easel-type legs. There is nothing else in the room.

Then, to the right of me appears another version of me, looking into an exact same mirror. I have the sense that I am the wiser of the two Brendas, that I have something to teach my 'younger' self next to me. I am teaching my 'less conscious' self about the people in the mirrors – our reflections - and helping her to practice looking.

But young Brenda is giggling nervously as she looks at her reflection. She is also afraid. She is young and new. I am old and knowing.

I look deep into my reflection in my mirror. As I look deeper, my reflection slowly turns its head a little, without me doing so, and smiles back at me, always holding my eyes. I understand that my reflection is another version of me, standing looking back, but I have to really concentrate to see this. If I don't look deeply enough I just see myself as I would in any other mirror.

And so, I am trying to teach my younger self to do the same, but in her own mirror. I am explaining that if we focus hard and look deeply at our reflections, we can see that there is more than one of us.

But young Brenda is still afraid. She tells me that she doesn't like what she sees in her mirror. So I move to stand behind her, to see what she is seeing.

In young Brenda's mirror I see a dark, fuzzy outlined face with no distinguishable features. Now I can see why my younger self is frightened.

But I am not afraid. I understand.

I say "Don't worry. Just look again. There's nothing to be afraid of. We must look after her."

And I go back to my mirror.

We look again at our reflections. And there we are, the four of us. All the same, all unique.

When I woke up from this dream, my first thoughts were "There is more than one of us. We live in multidimensions. We are One."

The Fledgling and the Dancer

It is a Saturday afternoon, December 2014. I am upset. I have had a realisation that morning about myself and the way that I behave and I want to understand this better. So I go intentionally to the Glade looking for answers and comfort. I really need some help today from my Higher Self. I go upstairs to our bedroom at ten past three, telling Dave that I will be back down by half past so that we can take Fig out for her walk.

At the same time as I visit the Glade (which I am seeing more literally today as somewhere above my right shoulder), I am also imagining that I am cradling a tiny baby bird in my left hand, holding her against my belly. The baby bird represents my fear and pain – the 'issue' about myself that I have come to the Glade to face and care for.

It is dark in *the Glade* today. Only embers smouldering in the fire. Standing in front of the log-seat on the right is Little Brenda. This time I seem to be about eight or nine years old. Little Brenda is wearing a beautiful sparkling silver-white long-sleeved dress, that shimmers in a smooth and fluid way from her shoulders to the ground. She has straight dark hair with a fringe, cut in a long page-boy style to her shoulders. Cupped in her hands is a tiny bluebird, flapping its delicate wings. Little Brenda lifts her hands to show me.

Sitting on my bed, I look down at my baby bird at my side and tears roll down my face. I see my bird as a newborn, all pink skin and without feathers. My bird is weak and it cannot fly. She cannot stand and is lying on her back. She looks like she is gasping for air, dying. I feel so sad and sorry for her.

But Little Brenda in *the Glade* says "No," very gently but firmly. She is telling me that I've got it wrong, that I've misunderstood somehow.

"This little bird is your freedom," she says, indicating her bluebird. "See how she flies. See how she dances and sings."

And the tiny bluebird in Little Brenda's hands flutters upwards, light as a feather and hovers just above her.

I realise that Little Brenda's dancing bird represents my freedom to *be*. My freedom to be *authentically me*, without the fear of negative repercussions if I ever make a mistake.

Back on the bed, I look down at my own little bird, cradled by my side. She is up now and moving around on my hand. She has fluffy downy feathers and is flexing her wings. My little fledgling. Not yet ready to fly, but trying. She hops up and down on my hand, chirruping, flapping and stretching. She's feisty now. My determined little one.

I look up again at Little Brenda in *the Glade*. Little Brenda lifts her arm and her bluebird is now perched on her outstretched finger. The bluebird jumps up and down, hovering and singing, dancing happily.

Our birds are one and the same. Only mine is still learning to dance, still learning to fly.

I came out of this vision with such a sense of peaceful self-acceptance. Tears still in my eyes, but a smile of understanding and gratitude on my lips. It was exactly half past three.

The issue I was tackling here in the Glade was about making mistakes and saying sorry. Apologising has always been difficult for me, because to say sorry would be to admit that I am in the wrong, that I'd made a mistake. In the past it had not been safe for me to make mistakes and so even when I knew I was in the wrong, I was frightened to own up to it, because of my fear of negative repercussions. And for forty-nine years I'd been living my life with this burden, up until this experience liberated me. My own children have, in the past, helpfully pointed out to me my reluctance to say sorry, but it wasn't until I made a mistake and didn't apologise for it this particular Saturday morning that the penny finally dropped for me.

This experience in the Glade helped me to understand where my fear was coming from and to accept and care for this wounded part of myself, like a tiny bird needing the nourishment of my attention and my love in order to grow. I realise that it is only by facing up to and accepting this 'shadow'[8] part of myself, understanding, integrating and loving it unconditionally, that I can become whole and fulfil my true potential.

The Well

For as long as I can remember, I have imagined the calendar year as a crescent, the curve edge of a capital letter D, but with a more open arc. January is at the bottom, and the curve is sectioned off evenly between the twelve months, ending in December at the top. And so, there has always been, in my mind, a huge gap between the end of December of one year and the beginning of January of the next, with the space in between an empty void, black, deep like outer space. Along with this image in my mind, I've always felt a sense of gloom and foreboding about this time of year. My birthday is December 31st. I have been uneasy about this distance between my birthday and New Year's Day. And I have never liked the first week of January. It's not a serious sense of anxiety that I feel, more a low-level sense of malaise. I feel better as the weeks go by and I look forward to February – a positively cheerful month to my mind. I suppose over the years I have put this down to the usual 'January blues' that everybody feels after the jollity of Christmas and New Year. But for some reason I have had the sense that for me there was another reason for my disquiet.

So, with my birthday approaching in December 2011, I decided to ask Suki, as a manifestation of my Higher Self, to help me understand.

Relaxed in shivasana, I go to *the Glade*. But I don't see Suki there. Instead I see something like a wooden-clad shaft going into the ground where the log fire would've normally been. The light is dull in *the Glade*, the sky overcast and threatening rain, but I can still see that the shaft ends in a dark hole pinpoint, deep in the ground. I hear someone say the name Freddy and then, in an unpleasant voice they say "I look ugly when I'm dead". I feel there is a question about who should go down into the shaft. I have the sense that I am Freddy. The other voice-person is really nasty-sounding, but the voice seems to be coming out of me too. Is that me speaking?

It was about this time that my counselling sessions with Sally-Ann were coming to an end. But we had agreed to carry on seeing each other to try out some matrix reimprinting at the beginning of 2012.

We decided to explore the experience I had had with Freddy. So, with Sally-Ann this time, I went, in my mind, back to where I was Freddy, looking at the wooden-clad shaft in the ground.

I am in a garden. It is night. I am standing next to a wooden-clad well. It looks like an inverted church spire, sunken into the ground. It appears bottomless to me in the pitch black. I am a young man, tall and dark-haired with a pallid face. To the right of me stands my neighbour. He is a man known to our family, aged about sixty, short, wiry, olive-skinned and balding. He isn't a nice-looking man – I feel something mean and pinched about him, something vicious. He indicates to me that I have to go down into the well. I don't want to as I cannot see the bottom.

"Why do I have to go?" I ask. I am scared.

"Because I look ugly when I'm dead," is my neighbour's brutal reply.

I look from the shaft to my neighbour and back down into the darkness of the well. I have an overwhelming feeling of reluctance and dread. I don't want to jump in. My neighbour assures me that the well isn't deep and that it will be safe for me to hide there. He explains that it is boarded up a few feet down where we cannot see it, so I won't fall to the bottom. But I don't want to jump in. I don't trust him. I am scared of falling, scared that the fall will break my legs.

I come back into the room with Sally-Ann.

We then worked together with the matrix reimprinting technique to change this memory into a better one, to help me get over my 'fear of falling'.

I go back into the scene. This time it isn't the nasty neighbour waiting for me by the well. It is my father, balding and around sixty. He is there, with his kind well-meaning face. I trust him. He asks me to hurry into the shed at the side of the garden. At the back of the shed is a wooden panel which turns out to be a hidden door. Holding up a torch, my father opens the door for me to show me a passageway beyond. The tunnel goes underground, sloping away gently to a safe hidey-hole, where there is food, a lantern and blankets neatly folded on the ground. My father tells me that I will be safe here until I can be rescued and taken to safety.

Sally-Ann then asked me to create a different future for Freddy, where I am safe and happy.

I see myself in America. It is the 1950s. I am a Hasidic Jew. I am fat with a big pot belly! I am wealthy. I have a wife and two young children. We are eating dinner. It is a party and we are joined by my brothers and sisters. I am the eldest and my siblings are much younger than me. We are all seated around a large dark-wood polished table, laid out with shining silver cutlery. There is a chandelier and deep red velvet curtains. We are laughing and happy together.

December

November

October

September

August

July

June

May

April

March

February

January

I come out of this scene and realise then that the Freddy I had originally remembered didn't survive the war. His neighbour betrayed him to the Nazis after luring him to the well. Freddy was caught, stuck at the bottom, his legs broken. Freddy's family didn't survive the war either, but Freddy doesn't know what happened to them.

My Grandfather, Horatio Bruzon, was in the resistance against General Franco during the Spanish civil war. I remember being told by my father that Horatio was a 'great orator', used to speaking in front of crowds of people and campaigning against Franco's fascist regime. Horatio was nearly murdered by a firing squad in Tangiers - punishment for speaking out against the dictatorship, but was saved at the last minute thanks to his Gibraltarian-British dual nationality. The Bruzon family, including my father, then fled Tangiers for Gibraltar, from where they were later evacuated to London. I tell Sally-Ann this part of our family history, and she wondered if I might be a 'cycle-breaker'.

I thought that the way I see the calendar year might change after this session with Sally-Ann. I expected the image in my mind's eye to turn into a circle, December and January united. But in fact there has not been any such shift. I still see the extended crescent shape with January and December at each end. But the 'distance' between New Year's Eve and New Year's Day has lost its sense of foreboding for me. I have hardly noticed it the last few years. And if I do think of it, my mind now switches to happy Freddy, fat and jolly, living his well-to-do American life with his family all around him. I am aware of what happened to original Freddy, but it doesn't frighten me or cause me any disquiet. I accept it, and I know at the same time that I have chosen an alternative reality for him.

It is my understanding that the past, present and future co-exist in our minds – the past in our memories and the future in our imagination, but that we only truly exist - we only really experience life - in the present moment. And so, with Sally-Ann's help, I was able to recreate my 'past-life' memory of Freddy and the well and form a happy and hopeful image of the future for him, instead of the one that I was unconsciously reliving every New Year's Eve.

The Crow

I walk down the slope into *the Glade*. The light is pale and silvery. It is the glow of moonlight. Embers smoulder in the fire. Standing by the log-seat waiting for me is a tall crow-like man, all glossy with blue-black feathers. His head is down looking at the ground and his wings are folded in front of him.

When he sees me approaching the crow-man raises his head. He unfolds his huge black wings, welcoming me. I walk up close and he enfolds me. My head comes up to his chest and he rests the side of his face gently on the top of my head. As I sink into his feathery embrace, I feel a huge sense of calm and that 'everything will be alright'.

After a while, the crow-man loosens his hold and, still keeping me close, we sit on the log-seat together. By the time we sit down, however, the crow-man has turned into a man dressed in long robes of light grey. He has fair translucent skin and his shiny dark hair is cut in a short angular style. He has one arm around my shoulders as he reassures me. I sense that he is an angel.

"All is well," he says. "There's no need to be afraid. All will be revealed to you in your own time. There is no need to worry. You will understand it all in your own way."

But he didn't communicate this to me in actual words. Instead he passed this understanding to me by emanating this as a kind of energy, filling me with a total sense of support, comfort and love.

After a while I leave the two of them together on the log – myself and the grey-robed angel chatting. I walk away knowing that this is a 'work in progress' for me that continues to this day. But I feel calm and I feel held.

This encounter occurred during meditation, the Monday after I had been to one of William Bloom's weekend workshops in London.

The workshop had explored different planes of existence, subtle energies and the different beings that exist in and around us, such as angels, spirits, devas, fairies, gnomes and elementals. I found this workshop very difficult. On the one hand I felt the 'blue pill-red pill' Matrix dilemma[9], wondering if

I was better off not knowing about this alternate reality. But on the other hand I felt cheated and sad that I was the only person in the room not to embrace this truth and not to consciously see or feel these other beings in my life. I felt confused and inadequate at the same time and I left the workshop rather shocked and upset, dazed but also amazed. I knew that I would find help and reassurance in the Glade and so I went there as soon as I could, purposefully and quickly.

When I came out of the meditation I wondered if there was any symbolic meaning for the crow in my vision. So I searched for "spiritual meaning of crow" on Google and I clicked on the first weblink that came up[10]. It said:

"The crow is a spirit animal associated with life mysteries and magic....It supports you in developing the power of sight, transformation and connection with life's magic."

The Tea Party and the Balloon

It is a beautiful summer's day. I am in a hot air balloon. I am aware that there are other people with me in the basket but I do not know them or see their faces. We are approaching from the right as you look from the ground, floating above a large country house with extensive gardens and trees around. We turn the corner above the house and begin to swing left towards the ground. It seems we are going to land.

Behind the house in the garden is a long wooden table covered in a white table-cloth. The table extends as far as the eye can see into the gardens beyond and has people sitting at it. I can hear them chattering and laughing. It's a party and there's plenty of tempting food and drink laid out for all the people to enjoy. I look down at the table as we sink closer to the ground.

I see my father sitting with his back to me, eating, drinking, chatting and laughing with the people near him. I long for him to notice me coming down in the balloon. I try to will him to turn around. I want so much to see his face. We come closer and closer to the ground and he begins to turn. I see the side of his face.

And then I woke up, still yearning for my father to turn around and feeling hugely disappointed that I didn't see his face.

My father died in 2007 after living for some years with dementia. I had this dream a few months after he died.

I initially sought the help of a counsellor because I was finding it hard to get over the death of my father. Time wasn't healing and two years on I was just feeling worse and worse, so I thought it was bereavement counselling that I needed. I discussed this dream with Sally-Ann. Sally-Ann suggested that perhaps it was not time for me to join the party.

Evolution of Visits to the Glade

Once I had finished my writing, I tentatively shared *Visits to the Glade* with a small group of my family and friends. I say 'tentatively' because this was the first time I had written anything like this and not everybody in my circle was aware of my spiritual beliefs and experiences.

I also mused at this time that I would like my 'stories' to be illustrated somehow.

This was in early March 2015.

Around the same time I met Corina-Stupu Thomas, a Russian-Romanian artist, now living in the United Kingdom. We were at a health and wellbeing event where I was helping out on the stand for my local yoga studio. Corina was on the stand next to mine and in the lull between customers we got chatting and hit it off immediately. Her stand promoted her artwork, which included a beautiful set of oracle cards, each designed and written by a different woman artist. The artists call themselves the Fearless Sisters and Corina is a member of this group. They are mostly based in the USA, but the group also includes artists from Australia, Canada, Holland, New Zealand and the UK.

And then an exciting idea started to form in my mind. I realised that I had been unconsciously gathering women artist friends for a few years, meeting them mostly through yoga and the home-based spiritual discussion group that I had been facilitating since 2012. Inspired by the idea behind the Fearless Sisters' cards, I decided to ask my friends if they would be interested in creating a piece of artwork for one of *the Glade* encounters, so that each 'story' would be interpreted and illustrated by a different artist. And I was delighted and astonished by the response! They talked of *the Glade's* joy and positivity, its beauty and the feeling of peace and amazement they felt when reading about my experiences. Some said they felt goose-bumps reading my words as they noticed parts they could relate to. They recognised age-old wisdom and archetypes and found their own profound soul messages in my accounts. It was then that I realised the universality of the messages in my *Glade* experiences and that these belong to us all.

Each artist then chose *the Glade* encounter that most inspired and resonated with them and this is the *Visit* interpretation that has been included within these pages. Some of the artists were so motivated by what they read, however, that they created pieces for more than one of the *Visits,* just for the fun of it! In the end, twenty-two pieces of artwork were produced - mostly paintings, but also including glasswork, fabric designs and a sculpture.

It was wonderful for me to see so much enthusiasm to create being born out of what I had written. Some of the artwork very clearly depicts my *Visits* as I have written them, whilst others have given my encounters a different 'spin' that I found both intriguing and charming. And in this way, the artists have validated my experiences and celebrated their importance through their own unique interpretations. I feel honoured, humbled, thrilled and amazed by their tributes and I honour and am grateful for the women who created them.

To celebrate all this spontaneous creativity, it seemed natural to me to bring everyone and everything together in some sort of event. So we arranged to have an open-house exhibition at my home in the autumn of 2015, to which we would invite family and friends. Our event would then culminate in a 'bring-a-dish' celebration supper for the artists.

In the meantime, in June, and facilitated by Corina, we got together to make a collaborative painting, to help us get to know each other better as a group whilst at the same time creating something jointly for the exhibition.

As the *Visits to the Glade* project gained momentum and I began to organise the group, I started to call us the 'Creative Sisters' – a sort of tongue-in-cheek shorthand name and a homage to the Fearless Sisters. But then happily the name stuck.

And so it was later in the spring that, encouraged by the response to *Visits to the Glade*, I started thinking that what had now evolved into a spiritual writing and artistic exhibition project, could actually be turned into a book. I didn't know how this would happen, however, as I knew nothing about how to go about getting published. But it was my fervent wish to have, at the very least, some sort of record of our project to give to the Creative Sisters – my way of thanking them for their involvement and as a token of my appreciation for their trust, support and acknowledgement.

And then in April an email landed in my Inbox from HayHouse – a free video series on 'How to become a successful published author'. I hadn't received anything from HayHouse for two years, not since I went to an 'I Can Do It!' HayHouse event in London in 2013. Yet here, in my inbox, was the answer to my publishing conundrum! I couldn't quite believe it. I remember laughing out loud and shaking my head in astonishment. And again I thanked the universe for providing.

So this is how *Visits to the Glade* became a catalyst for creativity, combining my spiritual insights and art from the Creative Sisters to produce so much more than the sum of its parts.

And as a result, *Visits to the Glade* as you see it now came into being!

I can only describe 'the *Visits to the Glade* experience' as a sequence of magical events wholeheartedly supported by the universe. How do I know this? Because everything has just flowed with absolute ease and fallen perfectly into place! For me it has been an almost effortless voyage of pure love and enjoyment and I remain both amazed and grateful. And I believe that therein lies the key to the success of this project. We did it for the love of it, with no other expectation than to create together joyfully from the heart. The love and the joy of writing, of expressing ourselves artistically, of coming together in friendship, mutual respect and support. And in honouring our *Visits to the Glade* we have been honouring and continue to honour each other.

Afterword

I believe we all have the ability to connect with our Higher Selves and the bountiful support and guidance that is on offer. It is my hope that *Visits to the Glade* will serve to validate the significance of these soul connections and help others to recognise the importance of their own inner wisdom.

I have been asked by some who have read these pages whether I am 'cultivating' my 'psychic abilities', as they have described my *Visits*, and whether I have had any more *Glade* experiences since writing this book.

My answer to the first question is that I prefer to allow the *Visits* to occur naturally. I do not feel any need to pursue, develop or control my *Glade* experiences in any way. These wonderful enlightening and supportive encounters come to me when I need them most and I trust that this will continue. But if there are no more *Visits to the Glade*, I hope I will not feel bereft. I want to live fully grounded in this world, not be looking to exist beyond it, or escape from it, in another dimension, no matter how amazing. I know that I have chosen to be here on this earth and that I have a purpose. I realise now that my *Glade* experiences are a wonderful resource and are helping me in so many ways to fulfil my purpose. And whilst my *Glade* experiences have become less frequent, I can now feel the gentle, more constant hum of universal connection within and around me. I feel loved and held and this is of great comfort to me.

To the second question I can say that yes, I have had another *Glade* experience, in July 2015. A very powerful and beautiful experience, as brilliant and nurturing as the rest. And this one too came just when I needed it, when I was in emotional turmoil and needing a boost from *the Glade* to strengthen me for what was to come. I have called this experience *The Star*.

I believe we can all make the connection to our Higher Self in our own uniquely personal ways. We just need to take the time to notice our inner voice and allow ourselves to let go and to trust. *The Glade* has been my gateway to connection. *The Glade* has enabled me to receive. But there are many gateways and ways in which to receive and we can each find our own way there.

Perhaps after reading this you might start thinking about your own path and finding your inner guidance. Perhaps you might find your own inimitable version of *the Glade* – your own personal gateway, or indeed gateways. Your own way to receive. For you 'the glade' might be a beach, a mountain-top, up a tree or in a cave. Wherever you just love to be, doing whatever you just love to do. A real or imaginary place. A place where you feel safe and enveloped in love. Where you feel free to receive the warmth of your soul's embrace.

I hope *Visits to the Glade* will inspire you to talk about your own soul encounters, your spiritual experiences. Perhaps you will write about them too. Maybe you will be motivated, like the Creative Sisters, to interpret *Visits to the Glade* through art. Or you might create something based on soul connections of your own. Perhaps some other form of expression may be born out of these inner journeys of ours. Who knows? I trust in the benevolent universe to show us the way.

Whatever you choose to do with your own *Glade* experience, I encourage you to share it. Share it with your family. Share it with your friends. Share it with the world. Together we can celebrate our contributions both as individuals and in unison. Together we can create a more reflective, supportive and gentle existence. Together we can shine brighter.

The Divine Light in Me Honours the Divine Light in You

Namaste

The Creative Sisters – Artist Biographies

Angela Parsons – The Tea Party and the Balloon

I started painting as a hobby about three years ago after having an interest in art at school. I like to work in acrylic and oil and keep my eye open for courses going on at my local art studio.

Brenda has written *Visits to the Glade* in a very descriptive way that brings each chapter to life. I chose to illustrate *The Tea Party and the Balloon* as I found a clear image coming to my mind as I read it. I am used to painting what I see in front of me, from photographs or still life. This is the first time I have painted from my imagination and I have found it to be quite liberating.

I have felt privileged to be part of the project and look forward to seeing all the chapters and artwork brought together.

Angela Parsons

angieparsons992@gmail.com

Annette Tickle – *Arman Safari*

I love all aspects of art and crafts and when immersed in producing art, I find my inner self. I am calm and focused. It was one of the things I enjoyed most as a child and I 'found the passion for art' again later in life.

I found *Visits to the Glade* to be very inspirational and beautifully written. When Brenda first mentioned about illustrating a piece, I was excited and slightly nervous as I have not done any art for about three or four years. I looked on it as a way back to recouping my love of art and being part of a 'team' who are like-minded and progressive.

I chose *Arman Safari* because I knew him. His family are devoted and loving and I feel he would have had tremendous energy and a pure, tender nature had he lived.

It is a privilege to be part of the Creative Sisters group and it has awakened a much needed direction in my life. I have a great deal of 'playing' yet to do to release the artist within but I know my journey has now begun again.

Thank you to Brenda and the Creative Sisters for this amazing experience.

annettetickle@sky.com

Brenda Bruzon – *The Assassination, The Well*

Channelled into academic subjects at school, I never got the chance to do 'arty things' beyond the age of 13. Later came making things with my daughters as part of their school projects, painting for fun during the holidays and making birthday and Christmas cards for relatives. More recently, I have enjoyed going to art galleries, on my own and with friends, admiring modern art as much as traditional.

Then came *Visits to the Glade* and the formation of the Creative Sisters. And amongst them came Corina Stupu-Thomas! With her iconoclastic and unselfconscious artistic style, she liberated me from the idea that 'I am not an artist' and helped dispel my fear of 'getting it wrong'. I was delighted to contribute to a joint painting at one of Corina's workshops and then later to our Collaborative Painting, at a get-together for the Creative Sisters facilitated by Corina in her home.

Around the same time none of the Creative Sisters had chosen *The Assassination* or *The Well* to illustrate. I guessed this was because of their 'dark' content. The images for both experiences remain very clear in my mind's eye and so one day I had a go at a pencil drawing of *The Assassination* in my notebook. A few weeks later I did the same for *The Well*. Then Annette offered me an art session at her house, assuring me that this would help *her* to get started on her piece for *Arman Safari*. And that's how I became the ninth artist for *Visits to the Glade!*

I have had such fun making my paintings! I am so very grateful to the Creative Sisters for their support and encouragement. Maybe now I'll have a go at painting the other *Visits* too, just for the fun of it.

Corina Stupu-Thomas – *The Mirrors*

I have Russian and Romanian heritage. After life under a harsh communist regime and the revolution that set my country free I rejected rules and sought colour to replace the grey of my youth. My paintings reflect my experiences, travelling the Caucasus, two day train journeys through deepest Russia to relatives, staging rock concerts in wild Africa - metaphorical and physical colour.

Painting intuitively helps me connect with my inner voice, heal the traumas of my past and help other people embrace a new way of looking at life.

Coming from a Communist country where grey was the dominant colour I rebel continuously against those times by using strong colours, big brushes, canvas and paper to experiment freely with various mixed media materials.

Getting involved in *Visits to the Glade* is the result of listening to my own intuition. It felt right and I did it! As for *The Mirrors* ... it simply spoke to me and while reading the story the image came to my mind so ... it had to be ... *The Mirrors* and no other story. Taking part in such projects, always brings like-minded people together so this is definitely the added value for me.

www.corinastuputhomas.artweb.com

Jane Montague – *Meeting Suki*

Fine Art foundation course at Manchester Metropolitan University.
Qualification as a chartered architect at Westminster University.
Work as architectural perspective artist.
Exhibiting artist.
Work as a therapeutic art counsellor.

My initial impressions of Brenda's *Visits to the Glade* were that I thought she wrote well. Then, that the account was intensely personal and it was a bold idea to get other people to interpret HER subconscious.

I chose *Meeting Suki* as it is the adopted name of my sister. For me, Suki, is not a name I consider natural for my lawyer sister. I was interested to understand and to depict a 'Suki'. I feel Brenda's description of her is much more what I would personally expect a person to be and look like, with such a name. My issue with the name, Suki, has been clarified.

I hoped that Brenda would be able to combine my painting response and incorporate it into her initial interpretation of her own dream. It is something similar to how I have worked, in the past, as a therapeutic arts counsellor; the originator and the interpreter both gaining insight into themselves and the other person. Brenda has not just invited me to carry out a commission, she has set up a dynamic between her inner world and myself, as an artist. A dream is not bound by 'reality' - it is much more expansive. I feel my world has been enlarged and hopefully it is the same experience for Brenda.

www.janemontague.eu

www.studiomontague.com

Jennifer Binnie – *The Crow, and cover art taken from 'A Spiritual Moment'*

I have always been an artist as I was born to artist parents, Dad a painter and follower of Rudolph Steiner, Mum a craftswoman. We were encouraged to paint freely and expressively and to make things from a very early age.

I had a formal training in Art and Design in the 70's and 80's, a 2 year Foundation course at Eastbourne College of Art and Design followed by a 3 year degree in Fine Art at Portsmouth Polytechnic. During my degree course I practised in painting and drawing, sculpture, ceramics, performance and film and continued to work in film, performance and painting after leaving college. My current work is focused primarily, though not entirely, on painting but in a broad sense, I enjoy the transforming effect of paint and colour and use this to paint on found objects, walls, bodies of animals and people, cars etc as well as paper, board, wood and canvas. I work with a range of media but mainly gouache and oil.

I was moved by *Visits to the Glade* when I first read it. I was moved by the honesty and openness of Brenda's storytelling and her interpretation of the visions. I chose to illustrate *The Crow* because it is the story that most resonated with me in a visual way. I have enjoyed being involved in the project.

wwww.jenniferbinnie.co.uk

www.artfinder.com

Karen Wilson – *The Fledgling and the Dancer*

My first interest in stained glass began when I was 15 years old and I went to Norway on a school holiday. We visited a Cathedral and on entering I was amazed at the light streaming through an enormous large round stained glass window. The colours were so vivid and beautiful, this has always stayed with me. I didn't take up a course until my later years when finally in 2014, I took a 10 week course at Sussex Downs College. I guess I am still a fledgling!

In 1993 I attended various art courses at Eastbourne College of Arts and Technology including painting, drawing, life drawing and textiles.

Visits to the Glade I found very honest and open. I was inspired to interpret *The Fledgling and the Dancer* as I saw this as an awakening of Brenda's spiritual freedom. I wish to thank Brenda for helping me to find that spark again in my art and to be part of the Creative Sisters.

Namaste

Sheila Glendening – *The Old Man and the Butterfly*

Since I was a child I have been keen on textile art.

I sold my first piece at nine. However I never developed this interest until I retired, when I did a two year City and Guild course and supplemented this with various day schools.

When I first read *Visits to the Glade* I found it fascinating and inspiring. I chose *The Old Man and the Butterfly* because I love the outdoors and wild life in general and a reflection of this enthusiasm is apparent in all my work.

I thank Brenda for giving me the opportunity to be one of the Creative Sisters and love them all.

Trudie Harman – *The Urchin and the Waterfall*

My enjoyment of being creative was evident from earliest memories of art, craft and needlework lessons in primary school. Enthusiasm for all aspects of art continued into A Level studies, the lessons for which were pure fun and pleasure. Any time spent in the Art Department made me forget I was at school!

Although not a professional artist, this launched a lifelong interest and hobby. I attended several Adult Education courses, including Watercolour, Mixed Media, Botanical, Historic Architecture and currently, History of Art and Artists.

The medium of watercolour remains a favourite. Random characteristics allow capture of subtle texture and charm, present in all natural elements, which makes it a pleasure to work and experiment with.

The Urchin and the Waterfall, described as one of Brenda's visions in her delightful literary compilation of *Visits to the Glade,* most inspired my illustrative imagination. Having a strong and intrinsic connection with the element of water, and all that is natural and tactile, I felt most connected with the ephemeral and spiritual aspects of this charming and meaningful vision.

To be a Creative Sister has added a new and special facet to my life. This is best described as a positive connection with those who are like-minded, giving me new artistic opportunity and inspiration, friendship and fun, all of which I value highly.

May this be the beginning of our inspired, creative and exciting journey together.

The Creative Sisters *(written by Brenda Bruzon)* – *The Collaborative Painting*

I knew all the Creative Sisters but they didn't all know each other. So it was a great idea of Corina's to gather at her house to make a collaborative painting. With eight others to coordinate, it was always a challenge for me to gather everybody in one place at the same time, but most of us did manage to get together, one sunny afternoon in June.

With Corina's enthusiastic and relaxed encouragement, the Collaborative Painting was started by each of the Sisters writing the words onto the canvas that we associated with being part of this project. We then dipped into Corina's Aladdin's cave of art supplies to paint, splash, drip, spray and print onto the canvas. We took turns, making layer upon layer of marks, turning the canvas this way and that to see it from different angles and encourage movement of the paint. As the paint dried, more treasures emerged from Corina's stores and we added sparkle and more texture with leaves, coloured jewels and gold foil. After a couple of hours of adding and playing, we came to a natural halt. Our painting was complete.

The Sisters who were not present on that day in June then added their parts later – spot the purple Pegasus, the butterfly, the white cat and the orbs.

It was an absolute pleasure to be part of this creative process and so freeing for me personally from all the perceived rules around how to create art. And since its creation, the Creative Sisters' Collaborative Painting has been much admired. It was one of the most popular of all our creations at the open-house exhibition.

Notes

1 Stepping Into The Magic, Gill Edwards, Piatkus 1993

Living Magically, Gill Edwards, Piatkus 1991

www.livingmagically.co.uk

2 Matrix reimprinting – an energy healing technique that has evolved from and involves EFT (Emotional Freedom Technique) to resolve physical and emotional health issues. For more information see:

www.matrixreimprinting.com

3 The Endorphin Effect, Piatkus 2001

www.williambloom.com

4 'pointing at the moon' taken from the Bhuddist saying 'the finger pointing to the moon is not the moon', as quoted by Eckhart Tolle in A New Earth (Penguin Group 2005), p.70, and relating to spiritual and religious teachers.

5 Meeting the Struggler visualisation technique, p.24-26, Stepping Into the Magic, Gill Edwards, Piatkus 1993

6 'This is Your Life' was a British biographical television documentary, based on the 1952 American show of the same name. In the show the host surprised a special guest, before taking them through their life with the assistance of the 'big red book'.

(Source: www.wikipedia.org)

7 Meeting Your Higher Self visualisation technique, p.61-63, Stepping Into the Magic, Gill Edwards, Piatkus 1993

8 'the shadow' – a term coined by psychologist Carl Jung, is the part of the psyche that an individual would rather not acknowledge. It contains the denied parts of the self that can become destructive elements in our lives unless we shine a light on them.

9 Popular culture symbols representing the choice between embracing the sometimes painful truth of reality (red pill) and the blissful ignorance of illusion (blue pill). 'Red pills' are people who have chosen to face reality, while 'blue pills' remain living in ignorance of the truth, whether by choice or because they have not had a choice.

The terms, popularised in science fiction culture, are derived from the 1999 film The Matrix. (Source: www.wikipedia.org)

10 The first weblink I followed for 'spiritual meaning of crow'

www.spiritanimal.info/crow-spirit-animal

Printed in the United States
By Bookmasters